Psalm Adventures: A Journey with David

David Emil & Suzeey Tina

PSALM ADVENTURES
A Journey WITH DAVID
Published by Aurum Writes Press

ISBN: 978-0-7961-5453-8

Copyright © by Suzeey Tina

All rights reserved. No parts of this book may be reproduced or transmitted in any form or by any means, electronic, mechanical, including photocopying, recording, or by any information storage and retrieval system without permission in writing from publisher.

Scriptures in this book were taken from The Holy Bible, International Children's Bible® Copyright© 1986, 1988, 1999, 2015 by Thomas Nelson. Used by permission.

Printed in 2024 in the United States

www.aurumwrites.com

David, the shepherd and musician, plays his harp in a flowery meadow, creating beautiful tunes that make everyone smile.

The Starry Night Prayer
Psalm 8

I look at the heavens,
which you made with your hands.
I see the moon and stars, which you created. But why is man important to you?
Why do you take care of human beings? You made man a little lower than the angels. And you crowned him with glory and honor.
You put him in charge of everything you made.
You put all things under his control: all the sheep, the cattle
and the wild animals, the birds in the sky, the fish in the sea, and everything that lives under water.
Lord our Master, your name is the most wonderful name in all the earth!

The Comforting Shepherd
Psalm 23

The Lord is my shepherd.
I have everything I need.
He gives me rest in green pastures.
He leads me to calm water.
He gives me new strength.
For the good of his name,
he leads me on paths that are right.
Even if I walk
through a very dark valley,
I will not be afraid
because you are with me.

The Songs in the Night
Psalm 42

A deer thirsts for a stream of water. In the same way, I thirst for you, God.

The Rock of Refuge
Psalm 62

I wait patiently for God. Only he can save me.
He is my rock, who saves me.
He protects me like a strong, walled city. I will not be defeated.

Psalm 30

Crying may last for a night.
But joy comes in the morning. When
I felt safe, I said,
"I will never fail."
Lord, in your kindness you made my
mountain safe.
But when you turned away, I was
frightened. I called to you, Lord.
I asked you to have mercy on me. I
said, "What good will it do if I die
or if I go down to the grave?

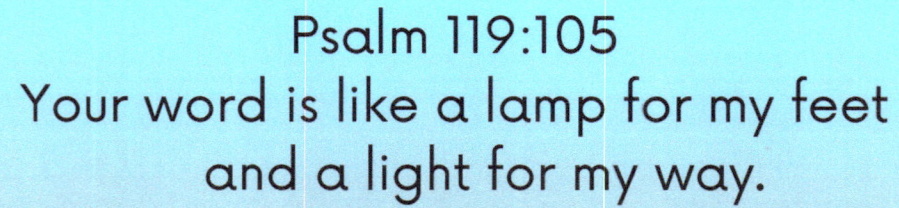

Psalm 119:105
Your word is like a lamp for my feet
and a light for my way.

Psalm 133

It is good and pleasant
when God's people live together
in peace!
It is like having perfumed oil
poured on the priest's head
and running down his beard.
It ran down Aaron's beard
and on to the collar of his robes.
It is like the dew of Mount Hermon
falling on the hills of Jerusalem.
There the Lord gives his blessing
of life forever.

Psalms 100

Shout to the Lord, all the earth.
Serve the Lord with joy.
Come before him with singing.
Know that the Lord is God.
He made us, and we belong to him.
We are his people, the sheep he tends.
Come into his city with songs of thanksgiving.
Come into his courtyards with songs of praise.
Thank him, and praise his name.
The Lord is good. His love continues forever.
His loyalty continues from now on.

Psalm 1

Happy is the person who doesn't listen to the wicked. He doesn't go where sinners go. He doesn't do what bad people do. He loves the Lord's teachings. He thinks about those teachings day and night. He is strong, like a tree planted by a river. It produces fruit in season. Its leaves don't die. Everything he does will succeed.

Psalm 98

Sing to the Lord a new song
because he has done miracles.
By his right hand and holy arm
he has won the victory. The Lord has
told about his power to save.
He has shown the other nations his
victory for his people.
He has remembered his love
and his loyalty to the people of
Israel. All the ends of the earth have
seen. God's power to save.
Shout with joy to the Lord, all the earth.
Burst into songs and praise.
Make music to the Lord with harps,
with harps and the sound of singing.
Blow the trumpets and the sheep's
horns.
Shout for joy to the Lord the King.

Psalm 27:1-2

The Lord is my light and the one who saves me.
So why should I fear anyone?
The Lord protects my life.
So why should I be afraid?
Evil people may try to destroy my body.
My enemies and those who hate me attack me.
But they are overwhelmed and defeated.

Psalm 103

All that I am, praise the Lord.
Everything in me, praise his holy name.
My whole being, praise the Lord.
Do not forget all his kindnesses.
The Lord forgives me for all my sins.
He heals all my diseases.
He saves my life from the grave.
He loads me with love and mercy.
He satisfies me with good things.
He makes me young again, like the eagle.

Psalm 150

Praise the Lord!
Praise God in his Temple.
Praise him in his mighty heaven.
Praise him for his strength.
Praise him for his greatness.
Praise him with trumpet blasts.
Praise him with harps and lyres.
Praise him with tambourines and dancing.
Praise him with stringed instruments and flutes.
Praise him with loud cymbals.
Praise him with crashing cymbals.
Let everything that breathes praise the Lord.
Praise the Lord!

www.ingramcontent.com/pod-product-compliance
Lightning Source LLC
Chambersburg PA
CBHW041200290426
44109CB00002B/80